Dancir

Dancing With Broken Feet

COPYRIGHT © Dr. Danny Griffin,
1st Edition November 2017
Printed in the United States of America

Dr. Danny Griffin
dwadegriffin@gmail.com
www.SpiritualMaintenance.org

Edited by Ron McRay
nonelbc@gmail.com
www.EschatologyReview.com

Table of Contents

Dancing With Broken Feet

DEDICATION

I dedicate this book to Dr. Ron McRay who edited "Dancing with Broken Feet" in its final form and to those who typed my earlier manuscripts and others who gave input. Dr. McRay is a brilliant scholar and author of many books listed at the back of this book.

I also with great love dedicate my book to Wade and Bessie Griffin, my dad and mom who daily lived a Covenant Marriage before us children and their world as faithful servants of Jesus Christ.

Finally I dedicate this book with love to my children and the many precious people over the years who have loved me and endured my brokenness to God's glory and my good.

FOREWORD

The pain of marriage is a reality that I have dealt with often over years of counseling and weddings. Three areas seem to afflict more pain than any other in the marriage journey. Adultery, physical and mental, the "Leave And Cleave," commanded in Scripture which infects and affects many relationships. It is absolutely essential that marriage partners release the emotional and mental hold that parents can have on them. Third is that weddings, no matter how elaborate the ceremony, and beautiful the words, do not a marriage make. I have officiated at countless weddings, but never a marriage, a concern of the couple and God doing business before and after counsel. Old timers years ago, told me of signing their names in the family Bible and moving in and on with their lives. A ceremony might come later.

I have done weddings in the Harvard University Chapel, Boston, Mass, and between the races at a NC race track before hundreds as it was televised, afterward riding with the couple around the track in a convertible. I've done weddings in homes, yards, barns, boat docks, church buildings and country clubs. Always praying for the couple counseled and questioned. Again I repeat myself, having learned over the years, weddings no matter how elaborate and well planned, NEVER A MARRIAGE MAKE! One could be "wedded" a dozen times and never have a marriage. Although It gives me great joy to celebrate the many weddings I shared in that did become COVENANT MARRIAGES.

Divorce is not the unpardonable sin but it is sinful and a sign of human failure and weakness. It is like a cancer and I hate it, but like cancer, it still happens! I have tasted its pain and hate every part of it.

Dr. David Bicker, my high school friend and student at Hampden DuBose Academy, is special and one of my heroes. His parents were missionaries in Peru and he lost his father in a car accident on the mission field at the age of 29. God has used him in my life, sharing many life experiences. As a college professor, he has impacted many lives and has been a great source of encouragement to me. He has been married to his wonderful wife for 59 years. Now retired, he reads and reviews my blogs. He sent me a letter from a young lady, and I have included part of that letter about her life and marriage.

She wrote:

> "The external hardships that we have faced have been really, really, really difficult and at times horribly painful to walk through. Some challenges

were really hard, like losing jobs, moving away from family, living in a city that I basically hate. And others have been incredibly painful like walking through the divorce of my husband's parents, the separation and reconciliation of my parents, losing a child, having a sibling walk away from the LORD, living far from family for a very long stint of time that I ever thought, etc.. I am thankful that the LORD held us and brought us through those trials, because in and of myself I am much too weak to have walked through the hard times and not completely crumble. Those trials have made us stronger individually and as marriage partners. At times I wonder if our lives were easier if we would be weaker or have a weaker faith … kind of like if you don't use your muscles, they will atrophy … so if we didn't have those hard times, would our faith have atrophied? Sometimes I wish that our life was super easy or that we could just do things we want to do whenever we want to, but I know that the challenges we face build character and perseverance, and most importantly the hard times draw us much closer to the LORD … closer to His embrace, and they force us to rely on Him and see Him work in ways that we would not have if those challenges had never come."

Pain and difficult times come to us all. Some survive and others fail, "Dancing with Broken Feet." I assume full responsibility for my failures and brokenness, while not adultery or murder nevertheless I am still needy.

Receiving God's love and grace, declaring as did King David …

> "Against you God and you alone I have sinned (missed the mark),"

but daily grateful for His constant love, grace and forgiveness. I am now far more sensitive to the pain and failures of others than ever before.

I wrote "Dancing With Broken Feet" while living 6 years in my office, having just returned from a second powerful life changing ministry in India, to confront the most difficult days of my life. Along with my personal struggles I did my dad and mother's funerals. This is not a book of theory and sentimental nonsense, but one of truth and reality. My greatest joy has been the many that have read the manuscript and responded with gratitude for the lessons of the journey.

So-Be-It!

WHAT OTHERS HAVE SAID

We are two Christians that each found ourselves in heartbreaking divorces. We both read "Dancing with Broken Feet" during that time. A realistic guide to understanding God's plan for a faithful and spiritual relationship. This book gave us both the strength and peace to understand God's love and forgiveness as well as His plan for our future relationship. This book is a must read for anyone in a relationship struggle.

Ron & Hanna Cescaline

- -

Once again, my good friend from High School some 60 years ago at Hampden DuBose Academy has just written this book that should be a blessing to all who read it. Dr. Griffin reminds us that there is none righteous no not one except by the mercy and grace of our Lord Jesus Christ. Divorce is not what any of us desire, but it does happen and when it does we need to deepen our faith and walk even closer with God. This is a book that can be of tremendous blessing to you who read it and I highly recommend it!

Dr. David C. Bicker, B.A., M. Div., M.A., Ph.D., Faculty Moderator and Founding Chair of the Department of Communication Studies at Arusa Pacific University.

Danny Griffin cuts through the fluff to address the areas people are facing in the real world. His unique style and spiritual insights brings new understanding to dealing with issues all couples face in marital relationships. Read this book! You will be glad you did.

Renee Coates Scheidt, RENEE MINISTRIES, Inc

"Dancing with Broken Feet" is an awesome read. Having "been there done that," I wish I had read this years ago when my first marriage failed. It answers all those questions you do not know to ask, as well as the questions to which you think are no answers. IF YOU HAVE BEEN BLESSED TO HAVE A GREAT MARRIAGE, THIS WILL HELP YOU MINISTER TO THOSE WHO HAVE NOT BEEN SO BLESSED. Danny has a very practical, down to earth approach to his teaching as well as his writing. THIS IS A MUST READ.

Ann Marie Fairchild - Christ for the World Inc, Lighthouse World Ministry, The Voice of Reason, Giggle and Grow Productions, Ann Marie and Jingo Productions

----

I have known Dr. Griffin all my life--literally--and he is the best bible teacher and expositor I have ever heard. He also happens to be my dad and my hero. In "Dancing with Broken Feet," my dad provides practical insight based on pain and maturity born out of personal experience undergirded by his knowledge of the Bible and love for Jesus Christ his Savior. This book is both authentic and *informative. Regardless of what you have experienced in life and where you are in your walk with Christ, this book will challenge you and help you grow in Christ.*

Tim Griffin, Lt. Gov. Arkansas

~~~~~~

This frank hard-hitting analysis of differences between marriage and weddings and men and women written with emotional intensity and passion produced a book with a thought provoking viewpoint different from any you have ever heard.

Thomas E. Waller, M.D., M.P.H.

INTRODUCTION

I wrote this book as a believer in Jesus Christ. The nonbeliever will also find this book helpful, as all human experiences are similar on many levels. The believer will relish the understanding of the Father and His grace, which is mankind's only hope. The single person will get insight into the struggle and human realities that are common to us all. The married persons who are on their way in or out of a relationship will find themselves somewhere in the pages and discover their faking, fixing and freeing postures.

We in this culture have often lost our way, with little concern for a covenant marriage, and a grace family with a proper balance of our spirituality and sexuality. This book addresses the whole spectrum of a covenant marriage versus the shadow marriage that mimics the real and creates the divorce.

Our problem as humans is not divorce, but gaining an understanding of what marriage actually is. It is obvious that we all struggle and many fail. Marriage and divorce after all is not a piece of paper but a relationship of the heart that either is or is not. Divorce is an admittance that hearts did not dance together and were left alone to "DANCE WITH

BROKEN FEET."

Marriage does not just happen, but is a mating of two hearts that willingly present their content to one another and dance to the music of God's grace and human commonality, arrived at by compromises and care. I pray that you will find yourself somewhere in these pages and be encouraged to no longer try to fix and then fake a relationship, but be freed to all of God's possibilities in your life, through His love and grace.

The grace family is our hope as we move from a shadow relationship to a covenant marriage and walk in it forever, processing and detailing each other's lives before the Father through His grace and truth daily.

A CONFESSIONAL PRAYER

I HAVE GIVEN UP, NOT ABLE TO COPE, LONELY AND TIRED, TRYING TO CREATE HOPE. NOT FOR ME, THE LIFE OF A CELIBATE MONK, PRAYING RELIEF, BEFORE LIFE IS SUNK - DESIRING SOMEONE WITH WHOM TO SHARE, LIFE'S SIMPLE THINGS, LOVE AND CARE.

THINGS WE OWN AND POSSESS, POSSESS US, NO TIME FOR TRUE VALUES, ONLY DISGUSS. ALL THAT WE OWN SHOULD BE SIMPLE TOOLS, SOON THEY MASTER AND DAILY OUR LIVES RULE. I HAVE DECIDED FOR ME, THEY SHALL NEVER AGAIN, LIFE IS QUICKLY FLEEING AND LOVE ONLY IS GAIN.

THE EXCITEMENT OF BODY TO BODY IS LIKE GOLD, IT MUST BE CONSTANT OR IT QUICKLY GROWS COLD. I DESIRE NOT STUFF, BUT THE TOUCH OF LIFE, WITH KISSES, HUGS AND TOUCH WITHOUT STRIFE. ONCE IN MY YEARS HAVE I KNOWN SUCH PLEASURE, ITS DAYS WERE FEW. BUT MY MEMORY I TREASURE.

TO FORGIVE IS TO FORGET OR IT IS BUT A DUMB GAME, SO TO DAILY EAT THE PAST IS A CONTINUAL SHAME. CHRIST DIED THAT SIN BE

COVERED AND FORGOTTEN, BRINGING THEM BACK AGAIN IS SICK AND ROTTEN. WALKING NO MORE IN THE PAST, I WILL LET THEM DIE, WE FORGIVE AND FORGET, OR – GOD'S GRACE DENY.

I LONG INTENSELY FOR SOMEONE TO SHARE MY LAMENT, WALKING FREE AND FORGIVEN, WITH JOY AND EXCITEMENT - SHARING TOGETHER THE WORK OF HIS GOOD PLEASURE, KNOWING ONLY HIS GRACE, DISPLAYING HIS TREASURE. LIFE IS TOO SHORT, I VOW NO LONGER TO STAY BOUND, SHARING MY HEART, TILL THAT SPECIAL ONE BE FOUND.

MY STRUGGLE IS REAL, AND I'M STILL ALONE, GOD IS GOOD, HE WILL DELIVER ME, GIVING RELIEF, AS ONLY HE COULD. I WILL GIVE ALL I HAVE, TO LIFE'S STRUGGLE WITH ZEAL, HE WILL PUT IN MY FACE, THOSE PERSONS WHO ARE REAL. I WILL NOT LOOK BACK, I WILL DANCE WITH BROKEN FEET, TRUSTING HIS GRACE AND TRUTH, I WILL NEVER RETREAT.

CHAPTER ONE

DEFINITIONS

"... in order that I may make it clear in the way I ought to speak" *(Colossians 4:4).*

DANCING WITH BROKEN FEET is a manner of speaking about me and all men and women who have discovered their sins and warts, and who KNOW that the grace of God has and will forgive all our sins, past, present and future as we walk with Him. Thus, all believers who have trusted in the death, burial and resurrection of Jesus, always realize and reflect on our brokenness and inability. We see our human imperfections in this body of flesh as "the treasure of God's grace enclosed in human vessels of clay, so that the glory may be of God and not of us." Thus, it is true of all of us that we "Dance with Broken Feet" and it is in no place more obvious than in marriage and divorce.

COVENANT is a binding obligation that God established in promise to us, whereby He became both the Just and the Justifier. Thereby, His redemption of mankind makes Him the payee and the payer. This is a Divine Covenant. The human counterpart is man, woman and God entering into a trust/promise relationship based upon their commonality and the processing and detailing of their hearts and lives. The missing ingredient in most marriages is covenant. The covenant marriage has nothing to do with a ceremony or a piece of paper, but it is written in the heart. This should take place before weddings and paper signing, both of which reflect a human contract between two people.

MARRIAGE is the joining of two people in contract with or without the State. Usually manifested in different forms in various religions or cultures (or both) whereby a man and a woman are declared wedded or joined. Usually thought of as the right to genital connection, that, in turn, produces children who also are then connected, by the law, to the State. Marriage can be just a legal connection manifested by theatrics and religious symbols and forms that actually have nothing to do with the true heart, spirit and mind of marriage.

COVENANT/MARRIAGE is a joining of man and woman in mind, spirit and body as a result of walking together under God's grace - a willful involvement of the mind and heart in the building of intimacy before the Lord and in the inner persons. Processing of each other's emotional baggage, past and present and detailing the spiritual concerns of the inner man out of each other's commonality builds the covenant upon which a true covenant/marriage is built. Penetration is a celebration of the mind and heart in covenant with each other and the Father, after the fact, not before.

FRIENDSHIP is the attachment of two people by unconditional love. A state of intimacy built upon honoring and cherishing - the primary relationship upon which all other human ventures are built. Covenant/marriage is built upon this factor as two become one by caring and walking together. Penetration is not nurturing in friendship until friends enter the covenant/marriage where it becomes a celebration of God's love and grace.

This concept is not in our time culturally friendly, but the teaching of Scripture!

GRACE is a free gift from God, unmerited and undeserved - God's righteousness at Christ's expense. The gift of God's righteousness is given freely to those who deserve the very opposite. While we were yet sinners, broken and undone, He came to us and found us and gave us His righteousness through the abundance of His grace and the "measure of faith" is to receive this grace. (Romans 5:17; Romans 5:8; Romans 12:3; Romans 4:5; Ephesians 2:8-9.) "By grace are you saved through faith and that not of yourselves, it is the gift of God, not of works, lest any man should boast."

SHADOW MARRIAGE is a form of marriage that is comprised of two people who have found no commonality, and yet, they continue to try and fix the relationship or to travel different but parallel paths, faking a relationship that does not exist. There is very little substance and usually one or the other is the strong one and carries the relationship. Their standard for the kind of marriage that they have is, "We've been together for X number of years" and that is about the extent of what their marriage consists. When the wife is the strong one, the children are usually raised by too many rules without much balance. When the man is the strong one, they are usually raised too permissively and out of balance. A shadow marriage has little to do with the heart and is very shallow and doomed to divorce, even though they may keep up the front out of financial necessity or convenience. There is no detailing or processing and usually communication of any kind is at a minimum. This kind of connection is very prevalent in our society and is very dysfunctional and unfulfilling.

DYSFUNCTIONAL is that which does not function or work as it is ordered to work - a breakdown of function which brings about brokenness and inability.

COMMONALITY is that which two people manifest in likeness of each other's thought process, reflected by how they handle matters and respond to life's situations. Commonality is an inner matter and a part of their make-up and temperament. Chemistry and conditioning are a part of it, and two people either have it or they don't. One should look for commonality from the beginning of a relationship instead of the "opposites attract" mentality that will forever frustrate and cause major problems unless commonality is developed. Commonality is not just "having common interests." It is much deeper than that. Commonality starts with the spirit of two individuals. If the two have commonality, then their basic makeup and life experience is similar. The outcome of this commonality is that the two share common interests and communication is more natural between them. "Doing" the same things is not commonality. Sharing the same basic ideals, beliefs and philosophies is. Commonality is very basic – it's spiritually and sexuality are commonly understood and shared, and cannot be contrived. You can fake the marriage with or without commonality. A covenant marriage. demands spiritual commonality. Opposites do attract and marry, working out their commonality.

INTIMACY is that which has to do with the heart and

inner realities; such as feelings and closeness that come from the heart. A sexuality that flows from the mind based upon the worth of the person. Spirituality strengthens the heart and enhances intimacy.

PENETRATION is that which refers to physical sexual intercourse. Because of health or age penetration may not be possible for either the husband or the wife. A covenant marriage is not built on performance as special as it is but on a love and caring far greater with an intimacy from of the heart and spirit.

SPIRITUALITY is necessary because we are flesh and blood, possessing the senses of touch, taste, smell, sight and hearing. We have available to us many pleasures within the range of our senses. Sexuality is not sex, though sex is a real part of our sexuality. Our sexuality is a gift from God and is a part of all that we do and are, thus spirituality brings meaning and balance to our sexuality.

CHAPTER TWO

IF I SHOULD DIE BEFORE I WAKE

"But by the grace of God I am what I am, and His grace toward me did not prove vain ... (1 Corinthians 15:10).

I was born a controller and a selfish soul, as is the case with all mankind. Men and women all express it differently – yet it is the same disease in both. These days, I can declare it more openly and honestly than I could in the past, but the pain is no less. We are all born broken and damaged, yet God, by His grace, seeks us and changes the configuration of our lives if we are willing. In his flesh, the pain and reality of our fallenness is always there. Thus, so much has been built around the corrupt self in us, rather than on His precious grace, making me a con-man by nature and hypocrite at heart. This would be devastating if it were not true of every other human on earth. The difference is in how we manage our own image, how much we cover up and how much we are willing to address. We are made by nature to hide our weaknesses and to pretend that we can set things straight, especially when it becomes evident that we are troubled at some level. Personality is how others see us while character reveals who we really are when no one is looking.

I have come to know my warts and flaws very well and have realized that my greatest weaknesses are also the base of my greatest strengths. If I were to die before I awake, this would be my last word and testimony from my heart. Hopefully, some needy traveler may draw strength from the realization that another pilgrim suffers the same struggles and insecurities. We always seem to have more knowledge than wisdom, and we can so quickly see other's flaws while totally ignoring our own. We desperately need to share commonality of experience and inner transparency, but most often we end up confronting broken-glass people who desire to hide the inner workings of their person to maintain an acceptable persona before others. This needs to keep what we really have locked up in a closet as our greatest sickness. Only when we can accept our failures, insecurities and limitations, do we begin to receive God's grace and forgiveness and begin reaching out transparently toward others.

As long as we fear that we will be exposed for what we are or are not, we shall be sick! Jesus and the woman at the well revealed a great principle of freedom. As He closed in on her confusion of five husbands and a live-in without condemnation, He simply offered her a drink of another kind, and she realized the nature of His deity and her ability to be released from her past. Declaring our sin, rebellion and brokenness sets us free from its hidden destructive nature, allowing us to move toward healing. That same woman went back to town declaring that she had met a man "that told her everything she'd ever done" and she celebrated. In that statement we see a freedom so few of us ever know. Her life became an open book at the hands of Jesus, and the pain of hiding was gone. In its wake was freedom to be a whole new person. Salvation indeed!

If someone says that I am a glutton, a drunk or a first class fool and I recognize it as truth, then my first cover-up reaction is to recoil with anger and defensiveness. But, if indeed it is true, and the arrow of reality pierces the armor of self, I can learn to be grateful for a brother or sister who dares to deal with me in such a transparent manner, holding a mirror of reality up to my illusion. If there is no truth to what is said, then we can but consider the source and walk in peace, grateful that it is not true. More than likely, what is said of us is a mixture of truth and error, because even as we are transparent with one another, we are flawed in our ability to see because of our fallenness.

This openness is not a normal part of our fallen response system, and it usually does not arrive on the scene until we have suffered much pain because of the deluded, proud nature of our flesh. Then we turn to a counselor or advisor who will hopefully help us hide our sickness and assess out blame, when we really know that only when our wounds are exposed, will we be healed.

Marriage, most of all human relationships, must have transparency and commonality. For, within marriage, all that we are and are not is so obvious. It is here that we must be able to say it all and hold a mirror to each other's flaws under God's grace for His healing. We must learn early in our emotional connection to process our baggage from our past, and to detail who we are to each other, so that true friendship based on reality can emerge.

Our children, time and again, will help to disarm our ego and will demand a hard accounting of our lives so that we stand absolutely naked before God and man. I therefore have no shame, because, like the woman at the well, I have been caught by His precious grace and stand a free man in the blinding light of His love. I often failed as a husband and as a father for the reason that I tried to do what I could not do. Posturing strength when I was weak, I ended up in failure. In my failure, God has again and again ministered to my life, setting me free to be transparent with all. As long as a person must protect his or her good name and image, they will remain hidden from one another and healing can never take place. Many an addicted person has said to me, "I am an addict." Detailing their addictions, they proceed to declare the need for accountability with others who struggle with the same addiction. I understand, for I too suffer similar denials and deceptions. Every man and woman that walks this earth has some form of addiction and brokenness. In our fallenness, we are devious of mind and deceitful of heart. The travesty is that when two people wed and become one flesh, they are still strangers until the heart of transparency, which honestly expresses human need and struggle, becomes the source of their oneness – the true source of covenant/marriage.

Divorce is not only a legal procedure at law by which a contract is broken, but it is the failure of two people to become honest about what they are and who they are. It is primarily a spiritual reality, not a fleshly one. Joining two bodies is relatively simple, but joining two hearts is a work of grace. We wed with too many agendas and unrealistic expectations, with little commonality and think wrongly that hormones will make the oneness factor work, when it cannot and will not. We must build our relationships on friendship that begs for total honesty, starting with the fact that we are all broken, hurting, possessing many failures and sinners by birth. We must choose to run straight into the grace of God and receive the gift of His righteousness. The scriptures declare with such clarity that mankind is by nature not good. These truths are self-evident to me, and in the knowing of them, we each become free to be a conduit of grace.

Now, I find myself under compulsion by the power and weight of the truth in my soul to pour my life out in my remaining years through my fingertips wired to my heart and manifest by shoe leather. Then I can care no longer about the selfish agendas and expectations of my heart, but desire to be spent by the grace of God. If I do not, I am worse than a man who has discovered a cure for cancer and will not make it known. I have made so many mistakes in my life and manifest so many failures that, without God's grace in my life, I would self-destruct. I can now only walk with those who are broken and restored by grace. Any attempt to explain or deny my flaws would be like an obese man who looks in the mirror and declares how good he looks while he continues to stuff his flesh. I am set free from bondage by acknowledging God's grace. Anyone who will love me at all must acknowledge that we are broken merchandise, bringing baggage, needing to be healed by God's grace. Upon this principle, strong friendships are made with other men and women as we join at the hearts, walking in the intimacy of love and forgiveness. This will enable us to function in the flesh. There will never be a marriage of any kind until commonality and transparency lead the way and God's grace rules as King. Thank God that now, on that premise, we can declare, "I AM FREE!"

CHAPTER THREE

LOVE / MARRIAGE / DIVORCE & FREEDOM

"... What therefore God has joined together, let no man put asunder" (Matthew 19:6).

It is obvious that we live in a broken, lonely and anxious world where we have been conditioned to love things and to use people. We struggle daily in this culture of loving things that cannot love us back. In this world we venture into relationships of many kinds, only to find ourselves torn apart by the pain of failure. Love, as translated by this culture, is conditional, shallow and unthinking. We have been conditioned to respond to our feelings, not to what is true and real. The relationships between men and men, women and women, and men and women have been programmed for failure from the beginning because we have been taught to wear a mask and to protect our own self-interests, rather than to give ourselves away knowing that hurt will always prevail.

Because we are all broken and so imperfect and frightened of transparency, WE DANCE WITH BROKEN FEET from the start. Thus, we build our relationships on externals and feed them with fantasy. We talk about commitment without submission, which creates even more confusion. Love that is conditional seeks only to satisfy its own traditions, which in this culture means penetration as the ultimate relationship between man and woman, satisfying only temporarily. Women have understood more clearly that they need to speak of (and reveal) their feelings that so often are masked and covered. Men, on the other hand, have been conditioned to speak of what they think or perceive to know, of skills and position, of how things work and what one does. This miscommunication is constantly closing the door on loving and caring. Love cares about what we are and who we are, not so much what we do and how we perform, our ages or what we look like. Thus, men with men can share the same agenda without knowing what the other feels, and, therefore, keep their image untarnished and their hearts empty. Women, on the other hand, share more easily their feelings and become more familiar with each other' needs and concerns.

When a man and a woman move away from the chemistry that often sets them up, they soon discover that no matter how hard they try, they do not fit together. They discover that physical penetration worked, but emotional and spiritual penetration of each other's lives never worked. Thus, sexuality eventually surrenders to the void inside the human heart that craves intimacy more than penetration. Therefore, in this fallen world, we have been scammed again by ourselves. True friendship is based on transparency, vulnerability, honesty and God who knows all that we are and aren't and still loves us. We must learn to open our lives to one another in all our relationships and their configurations. God and His grace come seeking us in our emptiness and need. He teaches us not to be afraid to reveal our brokenness and to dare to be real in this broken world. In doing so, we find healing amidst our pain and in our walk with other males and females, we are easily read and our mask is trampled under the feet of reality.

The primary unit of relationship structure is what we call the family – a male and female, bound by a sense of being one and interdependent, producing other humans, ideally encircled with nurture and caring that structures character and gives meaning and purpose to life. In our modern world, family has been stretched to mean any configuration of male and female and their children, whether by reproduction or adoption. The basic family in the context of scripture is one man and one woman under covenant. Thus, family can exist among those who join one with another, under the spiritual reality of God's grace, and manifest what is referred to as the "family of God." In the scriptural sense, men and women and boys and girls are brought together as sinners who agree that they are broken and hurting, sinners lost and undone in a broken world. Our commonality is in our basic character and personality makeup which must confront life's hurt and pain with God's unrestrained, unconditional love.

We live in a world of weddings, ceremonies and great exhibitions of high promises and happy talk which we mistakenly call marriage. God and His grace have so little to do with such performances, yet we have declared this as sacred as if it was God ordained and from His hand. We move from hot hormones to high ceremony into a house built by the hands of man and dare to call it marriage. Pious words and god-talk over the head of such will never produce that which is holy in a million years. Weddings are, by nature, performances that give the wrong signals and say the wrong things. One might wed twenty times and never know a marriage. It is obvious that reproducing after our kind does not make a marriage or guarantee a true home. Because we trivialize love, marriage and family, we always end up with the same confusing results.

Marriage is spiritual, while weddings and ceremonies

are highly religious and performance oriented. Once out of the limelight and off stage, the harsh realities of what we are and are not – dawns. And in the heat of this pain, we are overwhelmed and fight to keep the myth alive. Divorce is an admission of failure - that friendship never blossomed. Thus, often times, people in their parting become true friends, where the relationship found them only enemies. In the commonality of failure, they became friends. So, it should teach us that friendship blossoms in the soil of brokenness, honesty and transparency. There is no place more revealing of our gamesmanship as in what we call marriage, where the needs of male and female are never met because the ability to speak of our need makes us so vulnerable and we cannot speak our heart when so exposed. Thus, we continue to be unsatisfied and to keep the lie growing – blaming it on the sexes instead of addressing our mutual need.

The problem is not divorce, as prevalent as it is in this culture, but rather understanding what marriage truly is. We have sanctified a culture parade, process and performance and called it marriage when it won't begin to compute. The dating and wedding process constantly gets in the way of love and spiritual reality. It is no wonder that divorce eventually surfaces as the only option. Jesus declared, "what is joined by God, let no man put asunder." It is most obvious to those who think deeply, and observe perceptively that God has had very little to do with most connections of men and women. Thus, putting asunder is to be expected as that which was sown in human passions and heat is dissolved by the same. What we call marriage in this culture is more bondage than bonding because the spiritual heart is put to death by wrong understanding and misapplied principles in relation to what marriage is all about.

Beating the hell out of mankind with the scriptures will never set the heart right. Marriage is not a commitment to each other, but rather a submitting one to the other. Commitment is used most often to describe adultery. One commits adultery but submits one to the other in marriage. We have ridden the shoes off the horse of commitment. It has been more a door to bondage than the key to freedom. The spiritual root of marriage is grace and a lifetime of freedom that is based upon its renewal minute by minute. It is uninhibited and it sets us so totally free to choose to love, building a true friendship where intimacy is a daily celebration of freedom, joining our spiritually and our sexuality, which are gifts of God. Weddings are nothing more than a ceremonial contract with the state, whereas marriage is a willful coming together of two hearts that are continually set free by grace. Weddings introduce one to the bondage of contract that eventually beats each over the head with the law. Marriage, based on free hearts, is a continual celebration of intimacy on fire and friendship that releases the other to love; not locking them into bondage and control. One is pain, the other true pleasure. One will lead to emotional and spiritual divorce and deep regrets, while the other sets one free to love.

A grace relationship, a friendship, a covenant forever forgives and forgets, ever renewing the intimacy and friendship, acknowledging our inability to be anything other than fallen and broken with the need for daily renewal. The focus is forever on our common brokenness and God's grace and compassion, for we are sinners who share in a covenant relationship as sons and daughters of faith. What a celebration this brings to us all, day by day. We each should pray that we will build friendships for eternity and that God will give us a transparency that will allow us to be intimate and open daily to His glory. We can therefore learn to walk out our life with joy, laughter and tears, sharing the total spectrum of human life with others as we celebrate life and it's freedom, compliments of Jesus

Christ. Thank God for His love that heals, for marriage that allows two to make covenant and celebrate grace and freedom that is renewable day by day as we set our sails into the wind of His grace. The question forever and ever is not why divorce, but what in the world is marriage? We have asked the wrong questions and the answers, of course, are wrong.

Dwight Henry Small, in his book, The Right To Remarry, focuses clearly on the matters of divorce, remarriage and grace. The following three paragraphs are quoted from his excellent book …

"The church age is not under law, but under grace. It is not subject to absolute commands with legally determined consequences. The ultimate consideration is realized forgiveness, renewing grace, restoration to life's highest possibilities. This is not less true of marriage failure than of any other failure."

"Divorce may be allowed when spiritual values are at stake, the peace which marriage is to encompass, in particular. Marriage is made for persons, not persons for marriage, and therefore the person is never to be sacrificed to preserve the marriage. When the living symbols of the one-flesh union cease to exist - when love and unity of spirit no longer live - then dissolution may become the tragic moral choice - the lesser of two evils. To maintain the relationship merely to preserve the image of faithfulness along with legal unity when the marriage has died - may only destroy one or both personalities through indignity and unreality. John Milton called, 'God's gracious indulgence, the good work of parting those whom nothing holds together'."

"Let the church be bold in grace! Let the divorced and remarried feel fully accepted in the community of sinners saved by grace! Let the remarried find places of service in the church alongside those whose experience of the forgiving grace of God concerns less conspicuous areas of life. Let there be no penalties. Let there be the recognition of the necessity for the tragic moral choice in this world, the necessity, at times, of choosing the lesser of two evils. Let us rejoice that the absolute will of God is not compromised, but that He conditions the exercise of His will to our imperfect faith and obedience, to our sins and our failures. And may the knowledge of such great grace fill our minds and hearts with such responding love as will motivate us to attempt in every way to fulfill His highest will in the power of enabling grace!"

Only when we answer the right questions will life become all that our heavenly Father ordained. We have listened for too long to the religious, opinionated, dogmatic, proclaimers of deities and theology that have constantly enslaved us and put us in bondage. We must learn to read the scriptures under the guidance of the Holy Spirit, who alone can lead, guide and direct us. We will then, and then alone - be free alone!

What God joins will grow and grow; what man joins will forever come unglued and will be put asunder indeed. Once we have a relationship based on commonality, we must learn to look daily to Christ alone; who is the power of freedom and its overwhelming healing. Here and here alone will marriage become a covenant and our sexuality celebrated with joy and renewal and our freedom enhanced day by day. We must always remember that penetration is a celebration of what already is and cannot of itself, manufacture love, intimacy, marriage or anything else. [1]

---

[1] **FOOTNOTE**: 1. Dwight Hervey Small, _The Right To Remarry_ (Old Tappan, NJ: Fleming H. Revell, Company, 1975), Pages 137, 186.

CHAPTER FOUR

NAKED!

"The man and his wife were both naked and were not ashamed"
(Genesis 2:25).

"Heard the sound of thee in the garden, and I was afraid,
because I was naked: so I hid myself" (Genesis 3:10).

How we fear exposure – being naked – totally revealed. We cover our bodies with clothes, and, as our inhibitions go down, our clothes come off. Yet, the most difficult thing to reveal is our mind and heart. Broken man finds himself so complex and self-willed that he hides from himself and fails at communicating who he/she is to others. Man/woman was created to please and serve God who gave him/her life. Because of his/her rebellion and sinfulness - humankind moved from simplicity of purpose and pleasure to complexity of mind and behavior. Human behavior is highly unpredictable and very self-serving at best. Even when God is considered a part of the human experience, behavior is very difficult to explain. Belief systems give more structure to behavior but men/women can change their belief systems to accommodate their behavior.

Therefore, it is far easier to take off our clothes than to expose our minds, feelings and motives. Thus, when men and women seek to build a relationship, the sensual and feely-touchy process, once started, it closes down the mental and inner man aspects of a relationship. It is only after that process becomes more routine that couples are driven to discover who they are in the relationship.

Often it is too late to reverse their direction without separation or divorce or a long term loneliness and misery that comes with making the sexual, rather than friendship and commonality, the centerpiece of their relationship. Once again, the penetration mentality of our culture, mixed with a corseted puritanism, destroys not only the experience of intimacy, but the process by which intimacy is built. The bottom line is that we must learn intimacy and transparency, either before the marriage or after. Otherwise, the whole matter is doomed to failure. In this culture, that is spelled D-I-V-O-R-C-E!

Our hormones and erotic curiosity need no encouragement as God made us with a tremendous drive to reproduce ourselves. "Be fruitful and multiply," He commanded. This culture sells everything with sex. Our entertainment is loaded with its many possibilities, both normal and abnormal. Thus, from childhood our curiosity is programed and played with, until even small children in this culture are driven beyond normal interest and exploration into adult sexuality. This has dire consequences for a child's emotions. Their bodies become the center of their sexuality, instead of the process of total development, filled with proper structure, guidance and emotional maturity that magnifies the whole person, not just an act. Acts, as we know, become very addictive. Our sexuality, which is God ordained and a precious gift, is for our good and His glory. Yet, when out of control and connected only to hormonal response or erotic desire, it leaves man/woman scared and deeply troubled.

At the end of Genesis, chapter two, Adam and Eve were naked and not ashamed. No selfishness concerned only with its own gratification, but a transparency unflawed. In Genesis three, the very next chapter, sin enters the scene and nakedness becomes a problem. Sin is a disease of the spirit, a falling short, inadequacy which creates an inner rebellion, both passive and active. Thus, they hid, were naked and afraid. Sin today is still manifest in the same way. Because of the fallenness of mankind, we are all broken, carrying baggage that sometimes goes back for generations. We struggle daily with the possibility of addiction to any and everything. We are forever dealing with pain. Relationships based upon the right foundation can be strength if the two bond and bear with one another. But, because we live in such a feeling oriented world, we often surrender good sense and reasonableness for sensual experience.

We are not only creatures of genetic chemistry, but of conditioning by our own father, mother and kin, their biases and viewpoints about everything from apples to zebras. Their ways of thinking and personal feelings, whether expressed or implied, are transferred to us. The rest of our lives we either affirm them by repeating them or reject them by re-routing our lives, reconstructing new points of view and ways of life-expression. In the natural, truth appears very relative and absolutes escape us. Yet, in the physical world, gravity and the laws of the natural order operate on a universal absolute that dare us to defy them.

The word "naked" used in Genesis two is a positive statement of our non-neurotic sexuality, implying trust and total acceptance. In chapter three the same word is used to refer to fear and exposure. A relationship based on true friendship and intimacy always stands fearless and transparent in the light of the Son. As we peel back the layers of the inner man and open them to the healing love of God that is manifest by His grace, we are set free to love and be loved. God's redemptive work in Jesus Christ seeks to set us so free that we will allow him to love us. If the truth were known, God seeks to love us as we seek from our children and our friends the privilege of loving them. Thus, we reflect the Father's great desire and purpose for all of creation, that we be loved and love out of the overflow of God's gracious love, so freely given.

The nakedness of the inner man craves intimacy, and true intimacy is a product of transparency, commonality and bonding. In our culture, the pleasure principle has been our driving force. Yet it continues to fail and elude us. A relationship built on pleasure is, at best, built on a shifting, unstable foundation that is doomed to fail before it starts. Only a relationship built on the pain of hard reality sets up the glue that bonds "till death do us part." In our eagerness to get on with the sexual penetration process which flows from an overwhelming desire for pleasure, we usually marry one who is the least desirable for our lives. Thus, such connections are short lived, and what we term as divorce is inevitable. Usually the divorce takes place emotionally long before it is put on paper. I question that we should ever invoke "what God hath joined, let no man put asunder" to such shaky, undergrounded relationships which we, in this culture, call marriage.

No matter how much we "God talk" and assume piety, things that are not will never become without a work of grace added to each of the partners dance steps. We are prone, in this highly performance-oriented, judgmental culture to declare rules and models that are not from grace, but from human do-gooders who desire to fix everything. The phrases "traditional family" or "traditional marriage" smack of such self-righteousness that most of us who seek such a reality, end up crashing and burning in our own unreal world of performance. We either lie or become hypocrites of the worst order before the whole matter is resolved. Persons are special individuals who have their own set of struggles in life, dictated by chemistry, conditioning, culture and circumstances. Because this is so, each entity must flow from God's grace with its own set of parameters and imaging that nurtures and develops the individual marriage and family. Divorce is not the unpardonable sin! As individuals grow and discover who they are, as the layers of dishonesty and control peel away, they may join together with great joy and power discovering their hidden commonality, or fall apart to prevent further damage and pain to themselves and the family unit.

The healing of persons, marriage and the family begins when the clothes of the inner man comes off, as the pain principle cries for resolution and healing. The pleasure principle always wants to know what is done to deserve this, or why are you hurting me, and to attribute blame to the other, seeking to restore the pleasure that ceased. This usually leads to more pain and, finally, a bloody mess, as people seek the demands of an unrealistic principle and ideal that can never be met. The pleasure principle begins immediately in a relationship where people are seeking pleasures of many descriptions. The first conclusion is that we must get his or her clothes off so that penetration and pleasure can be fulfilled. Body nakedness happens, but it is not the nakedness that redeems and restores. The inner man steps out of his or her clothes and undresses the heart, taking up the dance of joy, intimacy, transparency and healing. Thus, body nakedness in this context, is a part of covenant celebration, fulfilling the scripture, "they were naked and not ashamed."

CHAPTER FIVE

"THIS IS NOW BONE OF MY BONES, AND FLESH OF MY FLESH"
(Genesis 2:23)

Marriage is the possessing of each in which each person belongs totally to the other. Thus, the two become a complete whole. In our cultural confusion, we have time and again considered this to be a reference to genital oneness which is in reality symbolic of the true oneness of the male and female who think and act from two totally different spheres of the brain, making one complete person – a completeness which manifests both maleness and femaleness. It is obvious that all the genital penetration and coupling in the world would never truly make man and woman one. Only a friendship that shares commonality and intimacy could truly say to the other person, "you are bone of my bone and flesh of my flesh." This creates the kind of caring that would never threaten or hurt the other – a covenant of caring that the modern contracts we call weddings and declare as marriage, could never produce. There is no greater pain in this world than to realize that we have said words and declared to the world something that does not exist.

To have and to hold means to behold and understand that a true covenant relationship called marriage is far more than the words of a pious man, in a quaint religious setting, with all the theatrics and trappings, or in a simple setting without the theatrics, with a justice of peace.

"Having and holding" is a work of the heart as commonality brings two people together as they process the details of their life and their baggage, willingly and joyfully. Again, we must note that the pain and failure of what we call marriage is set up to become a reality by the crazy, unrealistic expectations we exhibit in our complete ignorance of the nature of covenant. Preachers, rabbis, gurus, maharishas, priests, reverends, pastors or shamans can do absolutely nothing to assure a covenant of marriage in anybody else. We all, therefore, must be encouraged to understand the inner man/woman that exists within us, so that we might cultivate the principles of friendship and intimacy without the diversion of penetration and all that feeds that hormonal frame of mind.

To have and to hold speaks of a possession of flesh and bone that is connected by the mind and reality, not by flesh and fantasy. The erotic must be separated from the eternal if a true marriage is to transpire. What God puts together, demands that mankind leave it alone. The very nature of the inner man/woman relationship is unlike any other human relationship and most men/women never know it. Those who do must know how delicate it is and must never stand in judgment of another's failure. Yet, in this culture, when that which never was, becomes obvious and evident there are many self-righteous, self-appointed judges who determine that they know more than anyone else and set out to make a marriage by law and command when there never was one to start with. In this sick society we must never forget that just because the genitals of two people worked and children were produced, does not mean that marriage ever existed. When two people truly understand that being each other's flesh and bone, in the sense of covenant and friendship, nothing can take its power away. It is an eternal reality that is too powerful to be spoken of with words; and its caring and nurturing is not accidental, but deliberate and steadfast. We must never lean on the groaning of the flesh but the resolve of the will and the mind. Most of us who live in the West are the product of a free-wheeling, masturbating culture who never seem to move beyond that orientation in a lifetime.

Hitting the wall several times in our human

relationships we begin to realize what a marriage/covenant with God, man and woman is all about. That is why some people in their second and third connection of man/woman as husband/wife, finally learn what covenant/marriage is all about. Children always suffer and so do the parents, but, in this falling misguided world, it is obvious why. It is not a matter of whether two or three or more connections are right or wrong. Rather it is a fact of life with which we must deal, with grace and forgiveness. When a Volkswagen and a Mac truck collide, it is no time to assess blame, but administer help to the injured and dying.

Preaching at and judging those who have failed and never had anything but a shadow marriage is of no help to anyone. Those who stayed together for the children, or to satisfy parents, friends or kin, or some religious law, have often perpetrated a greater lie on the family. The children know and sense disharmony and become more disturbed and angry than if the two had faced their lack of commonality and love and parted, in peace as friends.

Many families live in the empty meaninglessness of non-existent intimacy, love or nurturing. Thus, children have been made to swim in a pool of indifference, hatred, anger and rejection by which their lives have been smothered, all in the name of keeping a "marriage" together when it never was a marriage. Remember, you do not have to have love or marry to biologically reproduce. We have beat the stuffing out of ourselves with the law of marriage that perpetrates a lie to the Nth degree. What we do not have, we cannot hold on to, even if by determined self-resolve we try. We either have a loving, caring relationship or we first deceive ourselves, and then perhaps our small world of family and friends.

Flesh of my flesh and bone of my bone is not wishful thinking, but a reality to be experienced when based on truth. Otherwise, it is fantasy unrealized that daily, anger destroys one's personhood. Most divorced families that stay together under the guise of marriage, do so to keep face, or play a game to appease some religious law built on guilt. They are driven to fix that which has no foundation or commonality. This totally denies the reality of God's grace who found us while we were yet sinners, "dancing with broken feet," unable to function. He came to set us free and declare our failure and guilt so that we might be healed. Thank God! He is a God of second chances, even in the arena of what we call marriage and divorce. We must never forget that divorce is not the unpardonable sin. The pain of marriage without commonality and covenant is awesome! This hurt needs more grace than perhaps any other along the road of life.

"Having and holding" must always flow from the intimacy of friendship and caring that results from the bonding of the minds and hearts of two people. Otherwise, having and holding will degenerate into two people competing with each other for the love of their children, friends and kin, pitting one against the other in the most ungodly of wars where everyone becomes a casualty. In the midst of this war, man and woman use each other to masturbate, often leaving newborn children to continue the anger and the war. There is no pain, no hell worse than to declare that one is bone of my bone and flesh of my flesh, it's at best a lie, and at worse, a total trashing of human dignity. We must never forget that sinfulness and failure are a part of the human condition and only God's grace can remedy the matter. The strength of having and holding is between the ears, not between the legs; in the mind, not the genitals. Sexuality between two people must be received as a gift from both people as they bond and celebrate their oneness. Two people who learn to receive love must surrender their control to each other. To give without receiving is to be in control of the other person.

Receiving is the most difficult matter we deal with in covenant. Because it makes us vulnerable and transparent as we allow ourselves to receive love and life from another. We must continually learn to joyfully receive the friendship and devotion that another offers. Then, and only then, can we declare that "this one is flesh of my flesh and bone of my bone" and truly mean it. It is then we can declare that we have experienced a "having and holding!"

CHAPTER SIX

LEAVING AND CLEAVING

"For this cause a man shall leave his father and mother, and shall cleave to his wife; and they shall become one flesh" (Genesis 2:23).

It is apparent upon reading the first three chapters of Genesis that it was God's intention that man and woman be monogamous, leave his or her father and mother and cleave to one another forever; emotionally, spiritually, mentally and physically. The more we understand the makeup of both man and woman, the more obvious it becomes that man and woman, in their fallen state, struggle with the most basic commands of God. If it wasn't for His grace, we would all be damned – one of the major problems caused by calling our contractual concept of marriage "God joined" is that we trivialize and romanticize marriage into a relationship of law and order, instead of grace and truth. Before the fall, mankind, in their untried state found their identity in God and His provisions. But, as soon as they fell, their identity became clouded and they found it impossible to leave and cleave because of the much unresolved baggage they brought to their relationship. Divorce happens because man and woman live in such a state of fallenness that they forever struggle with covenant at any level, and especially in the context of marriage. Thus, in the Old Testament, men had many wives and mistresses, and women took other lovers. That fallenness still stalks us to this very hour.

Jesus came to complete the covenant of promise and make it a reality once and for all. With it came a new dimension of grace and truth fulfilled and imputed to fallen man. Still, man stands with no righteousness of his own and inside a vessel of flesh. Yet, unredeemed in totality, there is forever the war of the urges and the deception of the flesh with its corruption and desires. This does not excuse man from human responsibility, but it realistically defines the reason for the struggle and war between the man and woman who think with two different parts of the brain. Thus, one of the core problems in a human relationship and connection is that man and woman never truly leave and cleave without intense cooperation from each other. They must share an awareness that when this reality ceases in a human relationship over a lifetime, the "marriage" or covenant is broken.

In this overly erotic world order we have too often concentrated on the genitals and not intensely enough on the mental, emotional and spiritual connection that is far more important. Thus, most people in our culture have never really left home. They bring to a relationship the baggage that still ties the man and the woman to the apron strings of parents and kin and ultimately leads to the destruction of the relationship.

Remember that the problem in our day is not "why so much divorce?" But rather "what is marriage?" Most of us, including those of us who cherish God's revealed grace through Jesus Christ, don't really know what marriage is all about. Friendship, commonality, closeness, intimacy, companionship and compassion are lost in search for the highly erotic, harmonic, genital penetration that has captured our curiosity from childhood. This drives us to a connection that can neither satisfy us nor nurture us in itself. We are always in a war with this fallen drive and must continually bring our understanding back into focus with man and God in covenant. Then, we can faithfully address the needs of the inner man and true spirituality which is the foundation of covenant/marriage. In these times, as the culture becomes even more broken, and men and women have less value and meaning, we must forever speak of true marriage as a covenant or we will end up trapped in a contract which will be broken, revealing the reality of divorce that was there all of the time.

Divorce does not only say that we as people have failed, but that the whole system of humanized religion and social rehabilitation has failed. We must emphasize human bonding and friendship without penetration. We have wedded and contracted time and again with no relief, love, compassion or direction. God help us! At the end of most wedding ceremonies, we would be more correct to say, "what man has joined, we pray that no one will put asunder." Yet, without time and bonding, knowing and growing, apart from the genital connection, we will forever repeat the process of divorce which is born the minute that man and woman say, "I do."

Instead of billing and cooing, kissing and petting, men and women need to concentrate on the caring, bonding and friendship factors that will build a foundation for intimacy and covenant. The "church" spends too much time seeking to re-direct hormones and the sexual/erotic impulses of man's fallen nature. This is absolutely futile. The "church" should clearly teach that the words, ceremonies, documents and contracts do not make a marriage, not even in the elaborate staging of theater which speaks of God and supposedly for God, so eloquently and ornately. Man is too fallen and so good at self-deception that he covers himself with pious, self-righteous fig leaves that are doomed to wilt before day is done. In order for one to leave and cleave in this culture, there must be, from day one, an understanding that the new unit of man and woman must never be invaded by the other's parents or kin. We, who are old enough to cleave together, must be mature enough to renew the determination each day to leave all, in order to become all that we can be. If this is not the case, no matter how much "God-talk" and piety surrounds the courtship and ceremony of what we call marriage - it cannot be and never will be a covenant. God never promised to join together that which is not – no matter how pretty or elaborate the packaging.

We must always be reminded that the emotional, spiritual, mental and physical baggage one brings to a relationship must be targeted and left behind. We perhaps will spend a lifetime recalling it but we must, without qualification, declare it dead as we walk in covenant with another. Unless we declare it under God's grace and forgiveness, we can never truly be joined except by theater and false promises that will come to an end sooner or later. We call it divorce, but God called it deception that was never allowed to surface and tell the truth. Many a couple in counselling have declared to me that from the beginning they knew things were not right, but they thought they must complete and clock in for a lifetime of misery and struggle, simply because it was supposed to be like that. Oh, what pain and misery we buy for ourselves. Yet, from time to time, many have encountered the exceptions. Men and women who fit no pattern, sometimes friends for a short time, a long time, a good time, etc., have met and walked away from where they came, never to return. They have walked into each other's life and sat down to rest forever in a loving, forgiving relationship – never to return to parents and kin except as visitors – never a desire to hold a grudge or bitterness toward their less than perfect mate/friend – always struggling and redefining but always together – never one without the other. Their one bonding factor is their commonality and, because of it, the lines of communication find ways to address their pain and struggle. Very few of us in this day have known such joy, but, amidst the pain of what marriage is and is not, those wonderful, rare relationships exist. Thank God they do. But they are not the results of human gimmicks but of a mutuality of joyous hard work as friends who truly love intimately, joined by commonality and human need and much forgiveness. I have met those who do not acknowledge God, yet live in the shadow of such blessedness. His universal principles and their commonality have worked just the same when discovered and applied. Too often we who "know God" are overly zealous and self-righteous with the knowledge we can muster yet we totally missed the reality of marriage, no commonality and joined by law instead of grace.

Leaving and cleaving is an eternal principle of the covenant called marriage. It demands eternal vigilance, for at any given moment a covenant/marriage under grace faces the fact that we must walk one step at a time in this fallen world where man/woman stand forever vulnerable and in jeopardy if they turn back to their former roots and baggage. We are too fragile as humans to pursue two different courses. Parents and kin must dare to say to their blood, go on, go on, be free from us and discover yourselves and become who you are under God's grace, sink or swim, but be free. We must determine to truly leave and cleave as a lifestyle – not an emotional, temporary idea.

CHAPTER SEVEN

MAKE LOVE! NOT WAR!

"... for though we walk after the flesh, we do not war according to the flesh. For the weapons of our warfare are not of the flesh, but divinely powerful for the destruction of the fortresses. We are destroying speculations and every lofty thing raised up against the knowledge of God and we are taking every thought captive to the obedience of Christ ..." (2 Corinthians 10:3-5).

"Make love – not war" was a cry of the 60's, and, often, the word "love" was connected with the word "free." For those of us who deal with human brokenness, we know that love is not free and, in most instances, is not real love but a cancerous, self-serving lust that destroys character, confuses the heart and leaves those involved scarred for the rest of their lives. The kind of love that builds instead of destroys, is that which is ordained of God and unconditional in its character and content. It is giving love which challenges us to grow and mature, not to pull us down and destroy. Most of us, so influenced by the spirit of the age, entered marriage with mixed signals about love. Where do the spiritual and sexual meet, and how do they blend and anoint each other with blessings instead of cursings?

We can remember time after time resolving to wait for marriage to consummate our relationship to be totally mesmerized by the flesh and its driving demands. Thus, it took character and strength to say "no" to the intense demands of the flesh. Most of us break, over being corrupted by such desire, that the spiritual dimensions of our lives are jerked around with much pain at our inability to "behave." Much of this has to do with our conditioning and culture. In the early days of our lives, our first connection with our sexuality affects us for a lifetime. Without some conscious understanding of our sexuality as we walk with the Lord and grow in grace, it can forever cripple us. Thus, God's grace must touch us at every level and set us free from ourselves.

We must always be on guard, therefore, to feed the inner spiritual dimensions of our lives with God's word and prayer. Exercising the inner man and learning to die to self, comes slowly because we resist the flesh's determination to control us. Our intense sin nature is constantly fed by the world order, our natural selfish impulses. We must always remember that the body needs air to breathe, the soul needs art, drama, theater, music, rhythm, poetry and prose to feed on, but the spirit of man needs quiet by which the inner man is quickened by the Holy Spirit, and grows and heals.

When the sexual and spiritual interact, there is an instant war because one comes from the flesh and the other comes from the Spirit. We must remember that our sexuality is a wonderful gift from God. The intimacy aspect of the inner man as it bonds with those we love, is non-threatening when it prevents the penetration mentality of capture and conquer to move into control. Making love is truly an intimacy question; when brothers and sisters in Christ and true friends interact, they are indeed making love. This is true intimacy. Having sex is a matter of penetration and is intended for procreation and pleasure inside a covenant marriage. A true covenant marriage is between God, man and woman. Without the God who "joins" on center stage, instead of man and his penetration and pleasure determination at the center, marriage and covenant hit the wall and a contract is signed with the state and covenant is lost in the shuffle. Penetration is to fulfill "... be fruitful and multiply" as a celebration of what is, not a builder of what isn't.

The having of children is a biological reality which happens, with or without love, with or without covenant. When man and woman are living a life apart from Gods joining and covenant, no matter how hard they try, they cannot create a covenant of love and grace anymore than bring justification to themselves. They certainly can change some behavior and seek to be more controlled, but without God's intervention and grace and a determination to allow it, none of us ever truly experience marriage covenant. Intimacy, on the other hand, is also a matter of grace and renewal, based upon God's provision. Men and women as friends should build all of life's friendships and interaction with one another on this foundation. Learning to "make love" as a daily way of life is a matter of transparency and accountability. God's grace should be center stage, allowing truth and time to make us strong in the "inner man." Protecting us from a wild fire sexually, that is out of control, and teaches us to grow in our spirituality that honors and cherishes the other person. We have truly lost our way and have, in our search, missed the mark time and again. Thus, friendship is indeed the foundation of all relationships and intimacy is the glue of grace that holds it together. Because human sexuality is of such high voltage, it can only survive inside the marriage covenant without disastrous results.

It is obvious that we have, as men and women, proved our "brokenness" more at this one point than anywhere else. Again and again, we seek relief and understanding only to fall back into a sexual nightmare that is without relief. Intimacy is making love; penetration is making war until the friendship and intimacy level grows into its full flower where both partners honor and cherish each other as themselves. Allowing God and His grace to dominate the touching and caring of human friendship when the aggressiveness of penetration is put on hold, allows men and women to discover the true hunger and cravings of the heart. When penetration is introduced apart from covenant, we cease making love and the war is on. Seeking pleasure and orgasmic fulfillment for ourselves is not evil unless it becomes the focus of penetration and is not built upon intimacy and covenant. We again and again continue to make war and not love in our fallen human experience. We have lost our way and our great need to love and be touched, will never go away. But, because "we dance with broken feet," we will continue to repeat the routine until we are willing to pay the price of true intimacy and friendship that honors the other person and becomes more concerned with giving than with getting. At this point, we shut down the war and embrace God's plan for a strong walk with the Spirit, no longer fulfilling the lust of the flesh.

Intimacy will always involve touching and loving, because we are indeed sexual beings. Penetration will always be a primary option because it is the easiest to address and generates so much heat and noise in our souls. Yet we, who are given minds to think and observe, must allow our will to be put under the control of God's Spirit so that we may allow our spiritual connection to be in control rather than our flesh. Our spirituality and our sexuality are both gifts of God; the spiritual must be allowed to dominate so that we can stay in balance and harmony with God's plan. This is a minute by minute routine and not something solved once and for all. Friends who truly love one another and are building a foundation for covenant marriage must ever monitor their hearts so that they may, with purity and integrity, define their walk and strengthen their intimacy and friendship. Such a walk will intensify their spiritual dependency on God and His grace and also will intensify their sexuality and demand that, moment by moment, we learn to say "yes" to God and spiritual reality and "no" to the flesh. There is no room for self-righteousness or denial here, but only an absolute honesty that continuously and clearly defines the flesh and the Spirit. The joy of making love, learning to "bear one another's burdens" and being there for each other's daily changes and needs will create a bonding and a friendship as it deals honestly with the pains of life. Once inside the covenant, the two continue a conscious nurturing of each other as the patterns set early in the walk lay a great foundation for the daily struggles inside a covenant marriage.

Making love should be a daily joy inside the intimacy of friendship, building the foundation for an eternal relationship – love without judgment, a love that cares more for the other, and a love that honors that person. We then must pray that we can learn to receive such love and realize that we are just as broken as receivers because we surrender control and our own selfishness to be loved by another. As we all learn to love and be loved inside a bonding that builds character, strength and purity, we lay a foundation that will stand the storms of life and the process of time. I pray that we all will learn again and again that we must "make love – not war" forever.

As friendship becomes covenant and hearts look toward the future of a relationship, this short poem reveals the hunger of the heart, one for another, in proper balance ...

"Come lay by my side,
Against my heart,
Sharing its beat,
Dancing with love.

"Share with me life's
Pain and pleasure;
Walk with me,
In the Son
Until life's race is done.

"You are precious,
Held in high esteem.
I honor your life as I wrap you in love!
Forever."

This simple poem reveals the desire to bring our friendship into a sexual/spiritual consummation – a desire to dance together in a loving, caring, giving relationship. The second part speaks of the reality of pain first, but also pleasure. The key is the walk under God's grace and truth. The third part of the poem speaks of the holding of each other forever in esteem and honor, loving and cherishing inside a covenant of love. Marriage of the heart must take place before the joining of bodies inside a covenant. The heart of true friends who move toward covenant will always know the tremendous pull of the physical, sexual connection. We are always human and flesh. But the control of loving intimacy is in the spiritual and we learn to yield to each other in honor, allowing God's grace and control to order our walk. When we truly love and honor one another, we seek only the best for each other. Sexuality is never more intense and on line than when it is controlled by God's Spirit. Never is love more powerful than when we honor one another in love. Divorce reveals that we have made war and not love – and we have lost!

DANCING HANDS

The most beautiful of all instruments of love – sensitive, flexible hands are the most precious. They bring that caring healing touch from above – softly, gently and lightly they are most gracious.

They walk with another without pressure or hurry, wired to the heart - they carry its loving pulse. Declaring ever so gently as they dance and tarry, dancing hands are friendship's connection so lush.

No violence or threat flows from loving, dancing hands, speaking silently of trust and care in love's passage. Going only where invited, carrying their tender message, caressing our many needs life's painful demands.

Observe friendships, hungry craving in the bloom of love, lovers and friends touch, softly as the cooing of a dove. People who are free from self, always reach out to tough, when the heart is afire with love we can never get too much.

Hearts preoccupied, careless and thoughtless are never warmed, selfish the heart, who touches not, no dancing hands to share. Satisfied the hearts need with shallow talk and empty form, chasing instant sex and shallow relationships leaves us unaware!

Dancing hands bring healing to hurting hearts and broken feet. Jesus touches us, and in God's time all things become new. Help us dear Father in this broken world to never retreat, give us touching hands that love and care – our hearts renew.

Seek, precious friend in this painful world, sensitive hands, imparting with grace the Father's touch, showing love forever. Our lives are so troubled with this world's hit and run plan, affirm, encourage, by reaching and touching in loves endeavor.

CHAPTER EIGHT

SEX DIFFERENCES
MAN TALK AND WOMAN SPEAK

It's true – men and women speak different languages! So different are our communication styles that it's almost as though women speak French and men speak Spanish. Each knows a little of the other' language but not enough to really converse. Here are some of the sex differences that social psychologists have found in language and communication style...

MEN	WOMEN
...talk about sports, money, facts, business and events	...talk about feelings, relationships, people and psychological states
...use commands to get what they want	...use requests
...use and respond to actions when communicating	...rely on and respond to words when communicating
...communicate to persuade, argue, control or impress	...communicate to share, inform, support or ingratiate
...use factual and action oriented language	...language is emotional and evaluative
...emphasize talking rather than listening in	...emphasize listening and sharing in

conversations	conversation
...use pauses in conversation for emphasis	...use intensifiers like really, terrifically, tremendously, for emphasis
...speak mostly in a monotone	...use a variety of tones of voice to convey emotion and meaning
...display feelings indirectly	...verbalize feelings directly
...interrupt more in conversation	...are interrupted more
...speak authoritatively regardless of subject	...speak in tentative terms, such as maybe, sort of, or I guess

By understanding one another's "language," men and women can communicate more easily and effectively.

CHAPTER NINE

COME LET US WORSHIP!

"Sarah laughed to herself, saying, 'after I have become old shall I have pleasure my lord being so old' ..." (Genesis 18:12).

"One has brought me to his banquet hall, and his banner over me is love" (Song of Solomon 2:4).

"When I found him whom my soul loves; I held on to him and would not let him go" (Song of Solomon 3:4).

"I am my beloved's and my beloved is mine" (Song of Solomon 6:3).

"How beautiful and how delightful you are, my love with all your charms" (Song of Solomon 7:6)!

Jesus Christ and God's Word came out of the East with its straight forward truth and graphic parables. It is obvious that God the Father created all things including human sexuality. All of its parts and functions were designed, developed and created by a loving Creator who gave to us this marvelous gift of procreation and pleasure inside the bond of covenant/marriage and He said it was good. Genesis 2:25 said that "...the man and his wife were both naked and were not ashamed."

To man, and then to woman who was taken from man as a helper, God bestowed the most wonderful of all human gifts. Next to God's covenant grace by which He declares us the receivers of His righteousness (eternal justification), our sexuality is a blessed gift to us, caught in the pain of human struggle as we travel through life. The celebration of our sexuality, by intimacy and then penetration, is given to mankind inside of a covenant marriage. This is done in order to protect mankind from himself as he involves himself with the high voltage of human sexuality. Nothing in human history has caused mankind more misery than his sexuality - out of control and turned inward as a selfish craving for self-satisfaction.

Man and woman, in their fallen state, repeatedly self-destruct as their sexuality moves full-speed-ahead, devastating everything it touches. The children of such unions bear the most scars of all, manifested by anger, depression and rejection. Man cannot fix himself or the fallen order. But somewhere in this out of control obsession, mankind must hit the wall. It is here that God and His grace find us all and bring us to Himself. There is no other hope but "amazing grace." Thank God that all families are not as dysfunctional as they could be, and usually, there is at least one person in the family who stands as the lightning rod for truth and stability, communicating some aspect of value and continuity. It was the man that God ordained to lead, teach an example of God and His grace to the family (Deuteronomy 6). The father should be the compass of the family, the one who lovingly and tenderly loves the woman and teaches his children about their sexuality and spiritually, and how they should stand before God and man. Only the knowledge of God and His grace can bring a man to this understanding. Without this reality, the family becomes self-serving and empty of meaning. It is most interesting that out of the east comes the most explicit, graphic depictions of human sexuality flavored with a kind of savoring, as if one was eating a many course meal. Our western, obsessed society is never at peace with our sexuality because we touted penetration and lost the capacity for intimacy and loving. In the process of having truly lost the "joy of sex," we have traded the mind and heart of loving and the caring of friendship for genital penetration, which is a fast fix and an easy way out.

While in India, I was introduced to the natural sexuality of the Kama Sutra and its tremendous, hormonal energy and its many expressions. The natural sexual energy of men and women inside a fallen body and in a fallen world sets the stage for wrong emphasis and total perversion. The Song of Solomon in the Old Testament is an unusual book of scripture. As a young man sitting in church services, sometimes bored, I would relish its reading while my father preached. I was certainly transported into a highly sensual environment as man and woman experienced a form of "worship" that was certainly exciting and breath-taking to my teenage mind. I was told by some that this was a picture of the church and Christ, but I was completely overwhelmed by the thought of the Christ and his church being so highly eroticized. In time, more honest understanding came. I understood that God, who created this most tender, precious gift of human sexuality, has given us such a beautiful picture of tender, loving sex inside the covenant/marriage, so that we might learn to worship the Creator and celebrate His gift as a wonderful banquet.

The wonderful book of Song of Solomon reveals the absolute joy, tenderness, gentleness and worship of God the Father Creator through the total giving of one to another inside the covenant/marriage. This must always start as a marriage of the heart and soul in intimacy. It finalizes itself in the beauty of the celebration of body to body by which man and women connect not only physically, their inner persons join in a song of praise for this most wonderful gift. Sexuality, viewed from this perfective, puts its focus on God as Creator, whose first command to man was "to be fruitful and multiply."

Sexuality covered by grace is indeed a marvelous gift for men and women as pilgrims and strangers in this fallen world. But in the hands of the natural man, that which is celebration and worship under God's blessing, is a curse of even greater proportion. Sexuality apart from the Father creates confusion and manipulation. Penetration and orgasms in the biological process may represent something for all pleasure and relief. But without the connection to the inner man, it is unfulfilling, and can never create the great joy and inner strength that it was ordained to fulfill.

The travesty in this culture where men are fantasy oriented in their relationships with women, is that the woman becomes another form of masturbation rather than objects of honor and esteem. In this process, men never discover their true sexuality and its purpose. The strength of man's sexuality is in his loving one woman completely, not seeking many to fill his fantasy and void. Man, pure in heart, has greater sexual energy and power in his purity than those who chase the wind and ever fracturing their mind and affections. Sexuality is not force for a predatory lifestyle, but under grace and taught by God, it is a symphony of praise and power. The "urge to merge" can be devastating. Our whole world suffers pain and brokenness because of fallen men and women and their urges that can pro-create and produce pleasure, but never character, healing and strength. When men and women come to the grace of God, they must learn anew who they are and learn to live out of God's righteousness. Living by grace through faith, in all areas of our lives, will set our hearts free to love and be loved. As we grow in grace in every area of our life, we will become more sensitive and tender. Those who are not in tune with grace and walk in other directions under the domination of the flesh or the old nature, will never celebrate the joy of human sexuality it its fullness. Thus, it is grace that teaches us that true sexuality is connected to the head and the heart, and our commonality and oneness will be enhanced by the work of the Spirit of God in the heart.

When men and women are connected through the heart and mind by God's grace, their sexuality celebrates this gift by reaching out to others who are broken and hurt. Human sexuality is fragile and broken, thus, man and woman must love from the heart and build intimacy, allowing the Father to walk in and out of the heart. We must never seek to create commonality for we only end up trying to fix someone and we only make a mess. Divorce is a separation of hearts that never were joined or fell apart for the lack of commonality or a proper foundation. Thus, sexuality became a chore and a bargaining chip, and its wonderful spiritual celebration was never a reality. At best, it produced children and temporary pleasure.

True sexual oneness is not a matter of the genitals but the heart. God the Father has given us grace that we might walk in intimacy, heart to heart with another. Those of us broken by failed relationships and unfulfilled sexuality must learn to wait on the Father to fill our cup of blessing with intimacy and service to others who are in pain. IN HIS TIME the blessing of friendship and intimacy inside covenant makes us one physically as we already are spiritually. Everything inside the covenant/marriage, the household chores and the daily routine of activities and maintenance, is done willfully, not for sex but as an overflow of the joy of sexuality and spiritually that is already fulfilled. Oh come let us worship!

We who dance with broken feet must learn to rebuild our lives and move in new directions as God gives us guidance. We must learn to maintain vulnerability and accountability, seeking always to build intimacy through purity of the heart. In a world of confused sexuality, it is most essential that we understand that God desires to use us as a conduit through which He can love others. God turned the force of our self-centered sexuality toward others. Empowered by grace and seeking to walk with one who is like-minded, as God brings to our heart that one with whom we should walk. Nothing is more joyful than to walk in a duet of spirituality and sexuality to the glory of the Father who created both and gave them to us as precious gifts.

We must never forget that the question is not, what is divorce and separation, but what is marriage? The place to look is to the Father. What man has joined, and I have participated in it too many times, never works, even when the seal of the state verifies it. But always and forever, what God has joined will grow and prosper till death! When God is the author of a relationship, then both man and woman will prosper, be fulfilled and be cherished. Then, and then alone, will we be able to sing, "O come let us worship" in relation to all areas of our sexuality, controlled by our spirituality.

CHAPTER TEN

FAMILY UNDER GRACE

Amazing grace how sweet the sound! We sing a song of family and grace, our lives under the Father's control. He is our glorious authority, focusing our lives on grace's reality. Addressing our inner man, we are renewed, lovingly accountable one to another, joyfully available each to the other's heart.

Hard truth and soft truth show us the way, instructing our hearts, teaching us to touch. As we dance, He heals our broken feet. Fragile and broken He found us. Unfulfilled dreams, broken relationships, He tenderly drew us to Himself. Our Father's heart sings of a second chance for all who trust Him and receive His grace.

Marriage is a fragile thing. Made for man and woman, one plus one equals one. A work of the heart, each cherishing the other, walking back and forth in the details of life. Pillow talk undresses the heart.

Table talk undresses life's tough questions. Pondering God's truth and life's realities, covenant/marriage sets the heart afire.

A shadow has no form or face. So a marriage without

the heart, the talk, the walk. We try to fix it, then we fake it because we just can't make it. Finally and at last, we just face it. Tired of pretending with shadow living, we free it to God's provision. Living in the grace family, forever free.

Irregulars and seconds form this family – lost and undone, healed by God's son, walking in newness of life, forgiven and free. Failures and disappointments addressed by His love; covenant/marriage a new way of living from the inside out, made by the Father, Spirituality and sexuality joined by His Spirit, two become one, shadows gone, joined by the son.

What God has joined no man can put asunder. Dancing with broken feet, dances anew. Forever to the Father we sing His praise. He has removed the deadbolts from our hearts. Together we ponder, share, give and receive, learning to walk with each other's hearts – conduits of grace, the grace family forever.

Danny Griffin

CHAPTER ELEVEN

THE GRACE FAMILY

"By grace have you been saved through faith and that not of yourselves, it is the gift of God not of works, lest any man should boast" (Ephesians 2:8-9).

"Have you not read, that he who created them from the beginning made them male and female, and said, for this cause a man shall leave his father and mother and shall cleave to his wife: and the two shall become one flesh? Consequently they are no longer two, but one flesh. What therefore God hath joined together, let no man put asunder" (Matthew 19:4-6).

"For of his fullness we have all received, and grace upon grace. For the law was given through Moses; grace and truth were realized through Jesus Christ" (John 1:16-17).

One who dances with broken feet inside of either marriage, divorce or singleness, must sail head-on into the grace of God, if life and relationships are to ever have any eternal meaning. A covenant/marriage is a different way of life built on the foundation of grace. At best, many believers in Jesus Christ have had shadow relationships and marriages that were just that, a shadow of what is real. Traditional family values and such terms do not speak at all to that which grace produces. We come to Christ from sin and total confusion, to truth and order in life and relationships. Traditional family values speak of a standard set over a period of time, to which believers should reach for and strive toward. The very idea in itself creates a sense of guilt and impossibility. Grace family values stand alone and build a whole new order in the life of a person. The new tradition in the life of a man, woman or child who come into the knowledge of God's grace changes the whole configuration of an individual's life. Thus, when men and women receive God's grace and forgiveness, they both will change. It is even possible that a man and woman living inside of a shadow relationship for many years might even go their separate ways to establish a whole new unit with someone else, when there has been no commonality or depth to the natural relationship. When grace and justification enter the life, it does not always bring a relationship together; it heals the individual, but not necessarily the relationship.

A shadow relationship, like a shadow marriage, is one that seeks to fix the other person or the relationship, and then fakes where they are, and then goes back to trying to fix again. The faking dimension is a form of denial and usually leads to years of dishonesty and more denial. This vicious cycle may continue for years, then, when faced, if there is a natural friendship and commonality, may come on line and become strong. Sometimes the relationship will divide because of the reality which grace brings. Sometimes the relationship will free itself and the two individuals will go their separate ways. It is obvious that we bring our baggage of chemistry and conditioning to the relationship called marriage. Unless we have processed that baggage and discovered who we are, we will be hard-pressed to establish a covenant/marriage.

The chemistry we bring to a relationship has a lot to do with certain traits and a temperament that will bring into this most intense relationship. Our conditioning is an even greater problem, continually revealing itself in the close confines of a marriage relationship. Thus, it must be continually dealt with and processed. It is absolutely essential to undress the heart and address the conditioning that comprises who we are. If we do not approach this most intense connection with the heart, it will develop a fix/fake relationship. Divorce is written into the "I do" of vows of those who have no root and no knowledge of who the other really is. This is the foundation of a shadow marriage. Because each partner neglects the matters of the heart and because they have no commonality except sex, they get caught up in the fast lane of activities, business and survival. They fail to deal with their true feelings and the concerns of a true relationship. Thus, faking and fixing becomes a way of life. Only God can fix us. If, by chance, one was willing to change his way on his own, in such a situation, it would only be at best a temporary surrender of individual territory to keep the status quo. Thus, allowing the pretending and faking to continue. Such accommodation and compromise of an individual makes one less than honest and only temporarily satisfies, eroding the dignity of the person and his/her self-esteem. Such relationships usually develop two separate, parallel lifestyles. Here the heart starves and cries, always asking for what it longs, only to be satisfied temporarily, and to cry again. Divorce already exists in this form of relationship, because nothing is truly changed or processed and the relationship continues for financial convenience and/or the children, who in the long run, will probably repeat the same errors in their own relationships unless the dead relationship is faced and freed.

There is usually one party in such a relationship that doesn't have a clue and believes all is well if sex and food are available, and the emptiness of it all is not confronted. The longer the pattern is allowed to continue and become entrenched, the greater the pain of the shadow marriage. The other party in such a relationship will usually settle into long term misery, not daring to stir the waters, until the one who has carried the pain of a separate, lonely lifestyle will either have an affair, if not in the flesh, at least of the heart, or seek a way to terminate the shadow relationship. Because of the many complex details of family, friends and security, many settle for the pain of staying in a sick or dead relationship. There are those who find the pain of leaving and starting over, less than the pain of staying, and they do just that. Those who are members of the grace family all have one thing in common; they have made wrong choices for many and various reasons and they have both sinned and been sinned against. When they begin their relationship, they may not have had a clue about the grace of God and covenant/marriage. But somewhere, in their pilgrimage, either one or both may come to know that reality. This alone will not fix a relationship where two totally different people married without commonality of life, goals and ways of dealing with life.

Coming to know God's grace will declare two people forgiven, but will not guarantee that a covenant/marriage will ever exist between the two. In some cases it divides them more, and they become even more different as they respond to grace and its healing in their own individual lives. They must then process their baggage under grace and move on to be free in Christ. They must each discover their place in the family of GRACE!

Now in Christ, man must seek his place in God's plan as the head of and the leader of his household. Under grace he must learn to be the cover of his wife and family. If he is beginning again in a new relationship, he will seek to learn to be strong in Christ and take the lead in the spiritual life of the GRACE family. He will learn to love his wife as Christ loves the church and to cherish her. At the same time, the woman is to realize that she brings to the relationship of the GRACE family her sexuality which addresses the man's way of life with great joy and pleasure as she teaches him to love and respond tenderly to her special gift.

Through this door, by way of pillow talk and communication of the heart, she helps the man address her life through their commonality. He with his spirituality and she with her sexuality, will enhance each other in the GRACE family as they grow together, learning to process and detail their lives each day. The fall-out will nurture the children and the family unit and the overflow will bless those around them. The tough matters of the family's survival will be addressed at daily table-talk, as they learn to address each other from the male/female sides of the brain; not with anger, but with love and reason. The GRACE family must walk daily with the Father and give great attention to the matters of the heart.

It is obvious that we have falsely believed that all that a man or woman has to do is come to Christ and everything will be fixed. Often there is a splintering, then a regrouping and then a healing of the two people who never really knew each other. There may develop a hunger to connect properly to build a foundation for a covenant/marriage, to establish a GRACE family. If there is to be a foundation to build on, the two must individually process their own human baggage and establish their own identity. Having done this, if they truly know each other and the ins and outs of each other's hearts with commonality, then they have laid a foundation for the GRACE family. However, if they have lived separate lifestyles and have not processed their baggage and walked it out, they have little to form a foundation for the continuance of the relationship. And, if the fix/fake cycle has produced only frustration without commonality, then they no doubt should free themselves and go their way to start a life with a new foundation and new dimensions, hopefully building correctly through the process and detailing of their lives. The GRACE family is filled with many and varied patterns of function and dysfunction that God breaks and then fixes.

Sometimes relationships are reformed with the same people, and sometimes with a whole new configuration of family. We have far too long used what we call the traditional Christian family to set a standard for the family. It has often become an unattainable ideal, almost a law of expectation that creates guilt when perfection is not attained. The GRACE family reaches out to all broken and irregular people who have come by grace through a bad marriage, a painful divorce, or other dysfunction and offers them hope. Grace calls all broken people to forgiveness and a new day and a new direction, giving hope to those who are broken and those who have failed. It offers hope to parents and children who come from broken, troubled, angry, impossible situations. Situations where they have grown up in shadow relationships, where hyperactivity has replaced intimacy and compassion, and where, often, one parent has raised the children and taught whatever values were taught.

Broken adults and broken children must know, as did the woman at the well in John 4, that they are forgiven and set free from their pasts. Fragmented people and fragmented relationships can be rebuilt after divorce and produce strong covenant/marriages under new management, with new mates. With grace in the heart, we can receive a second chance to build anew out of a brokenness and failure, becoming a grace family with a new direction and a new usefulness for the kingdom of God.

Thus, people who try to fix the fake, must finally face all the dysfunction and failure created by not having processed all their baggage. They must finally discover that God's grace frees their infected connection and helps them to forever escape the pain of bad choices. Now by grace, they must begin building a new thing, a new relationship, a new purpose and a new configuration – "amazing grace" wins the day! What God has joined let no man put asunder. It is obvious that God has joined none of our dysfunctional, foundationless, lacking in spiritual leadership, full of hot hormones, paste up marriages, complete with unprocessed baggage and shallow communication. These forms of shallow marriage are prevalent in our society because of our very shallow views of marriage. Remember, the problem is not divorce, but our wrong view of marriage. This culture persists in seeking to sanctify or fix relationships that are broken and unprocessed. From the very ritualistic "I DO," divorce is written in the fabric of our wedding form. Without a proper foundation of human perseverance and Divine grace, no covenant/marriage will ever be built.

Another form of the GRACE family is to be found in the woman or man who either has a weak mate or is separated or divorced. All of these have one thing in common, and that is that one parent is carrying the weight of child raising and family direction. These hearty souls with God's help and grace can do a good job, though they may find the job very difficult, unnatural, lonely and painful. Out of such families can come strong people and wonderful children, though not without tremendous effort. Such strong and unusual people require that the church surround them with love and surrogate role models.

Believers in Jesus Christ face the same human dilemmas that the natural man does. They face the same struggles with relationships, marriage and the family. However, they have the resource of grace in their lives with its options and power that empowers them to go in a different direction and walk it out.

Believers also can, and do, make poor choices and don't always build proper foundations, thus, their relationships come apart. Knowing God and His grace is not instant magic and does not guarantee perfection, or even success, in relationships. One must choose to allow the Lord to dominate the foundational process used in building the relationship in the hearts of both. They must exercise their willingness to set aside the hormonal/physical relationship, in order to build a strong understanding of each other's lives and thought processes.

There must be much prayer and all the details of life, individual conditioning and individual weaknesses and strengths must be shared. This alone does not guarantee a perfect relationship, but it lays the ground-work of a strong foundation for a covenant/marriage and a platform for its growth. A public wedding should not be rushed, but done IN GOD'S TIME as God's Spirit seals the hearts of the man and woman who are already walking in covenant/marriage in their hearts. The public declaration does not make the marriage a covenant. That work must already be done by God in the hearts of each.

The declaration before men gives witness and testimony to what God has already done. Ceremonies and weddings are mostly theatrics and do not make or break a covenant between a man and woman; they are for effect and show and cannot create what does not already exist. A GRACE family marriage starts and ends in the hearts and souls of two people and is built with much concentration, sacrifice, pain and passion. The GRACE family is a composition of broken, sinful, troubled people who have been found by God and His grace and have had their lives reconfigured. Sexual penetration must not be the issue in foundation building, but rather intimacy and inner discovery. After that, penetration and fulfillment are for the celebration of covenant and/or for procreation of the human race.

CHAPTER TWELVE

BUILDING A STRONG GRACE FAMILY

Once a man and woman are freed of their past by the grace of God, have begun processing their lives together, and they are ready to declare and walk out their covenant/marriage, they need to take special measures in order to walk daily with each other's hearts. A connection of the heart demands constant awareness built upon processing the daily struggles of life and its details. Thus, both man and woman must stay available to each other's feelings and emotions so that, in their commonality, they can address each other in relation to the male and female points of view on a daily basis. The GRACE family will thrive on a balance of spirituality and sexuality, walked out with love, day by day.

There are at least three things necessary in order to maintain the heart relationship inside the covenant marriage.

PROCESSING AND DETAILING ...

... this is a daily exercise of the heart, necessary to keep lines of love and communication open. It is a way of sharing all the struggles of the heart connected to past conditioning, dealing with the male and female points of view and of improving the connection inside the GRACE family concerning those matters both spiritual and sexual. This is what formed the marriage of the hearts to begin with, and will be the most fruitful in the process of GRACE family living. Praying together is an important part of the daily walk, and it always strengthens the hearts and lives of the man and the woman.

TABLE-TALK ...

... is a process of daily communications, even if just for a short time, but still very important to the health of the relationship. There must be a sitting down, one with the other, to spell out the needs of the family, whether it is to deal with a purchase for the family, or something to do with child rearing or some need in the relationship between the man and the woman, where strong discussion without anger and judgment can take place. Finances and other decisions, matters such as family direction should be discussed and resolved at table-talk. Disagreements and speaking one's mind are acceptable, but always in love, and never in a controlling, vengeful manner. Table-talk should always end with prayer for wisdom and guidance. Reading scripture and sharing is also a good way to end this time together.

PILLOW-TALK ...

... is on the bed or somewhere else in a laid back, relaxed, even tired, frame of mind, where touching and tenderness prevail, husband and wife in the GRACE family should share intimacy and love. No table-talk or business dealings are allowed here. This special time should address the inner needs of both persons. Spiritual and sexual feelings should be discussed and shared in a very protected, loving environment. Here the woman is queen, and both should use this special time to address the heart needs of each other. This should become a very special time inside the GRACE family, as the man and woman look toward this time each day. It is a time to renew their lives, each to the other, inside a spirituality brought by the man as a covering of the woman, and sexuality brought to the pillow by the woman who wisely knows that true sexuality is far more than penetration, but is rather an inner reality that addresses the feelings and needs of the heart.

As the man addresses the spiritual need of the woman, she, in turn, will lovingly address the feelings of the heart where true sexuality lives and grows. After the love making, whether verbal, physical or both, they should close the day with a time of prayer and gratitude. This is the wellspring of heart renewal for the GRACE family.

Because of sickness, child rearing difficulties or some unforeseen event, some evenings may have to forego or modify pillow talk. This should not become the acceptable routine, or both man and woman will suffer in the strength of their bonding. The other two exercises should also be done consistently, though sometimes they will be more abbreviated and at other times longer. If the family is not able to fulfill them at all times it should be acknowledged and not allowed to lapse for long.

The GRACE family demands attention to details as God's healing of the family is brought about by the man's strong spiritual leadership and the woman's loving sexuality. The balance and blend of these two things will help protect those who have lived through marriage and divorce and desire to never make the same mistakes again. These matters demand deliberate and determined effort so that the old patterns and conditioning from the past will never return.

CHAPTER THIRTEEN

THE GRACE FAMILY AND THE WOMAN ALONE

"For I am mindful of the sincere faith within you, which first dwelt in your grandmother Lois, and your mother Eunice, and I am sure that it is in you as well" (2 Timothy 1:5).

When a husband/father dies, or leaves, or is out to lunch emotionally, what happens to the wife and/or children? The wife/mother must deal with plan B instead of plan A when there is no spiritual and emotional support system at work in their relationship. Plan A would hold that a mutual covenant exists where the husband/father cherishes and honors his wife by providing spiritual and emotional support to the wife and family. In these days, this is a rarity and the wife/mother must look to plan B. This means that she must carry the full support of the family and bear the pain and isolation of it all.

In 2 Timothy 1:5, it appears that Paul remembers young Timothy, whom he spoke so highly of, when he says in Philippians 2:20 that he has "no one else of kindred spirit who will genuinely be concerned for your welfare." From this statement, it appears that Timothy had been raised by two women, for there is no mention of his father for whatever reason. In our world, the women must be the strong ones emotionally and spiritually both for herself and for her children. This passage of scripture should greatly encourage mothers who are seeking to be faithful in raising children. It is very obvious from what we know about Timothy, that his mother Eunice and his grandmother Lois had done a great job in raising a strong son with great character and dependability. Wherever the scripture speaks of God's standard for the family and the home, the father is given the responsibility of being accountable to God for the family.

In a broken world like ours, there are so few strong men that exist. The woman, by default, becomes the covering and the definer of the family. God always honors such faithfulness. Many great and mighty men and women have come from families where the mother carried most, if not all, of the responsibility. Our world would be far worse off and our nation far more broken if it were not for hard working, strong, praying mothers who stand in the gap and raise sons and daughters with strength of character, strong minds and sensitive spirits. God always blesses truth and principle, wherever it is found. Thank God for mothers who are faithful and committed to producing sons and daughters who become caring, loving, solid citizens in a crazy, broken world. Remember, someone has well said, "The hand that rocks the cradle rules the world!" The scripture is filled with illustrations of strong women who stood alone and made a difference for the good of mankind and the glory of God.

CHAPTER FOURTEEN

A FINAL WORD ABOUT COMMONALITY

In man's fallenness, he is given to living contrary to that which is both good for him and in his best interest. In the realm of love and marriage, man has repeatedly shot himself in the foot by his attempt to fix his life with the woman of his dreams by living agendas that will not compute. One of those agendas we have so often fallen victim of is the one that declares "opposites attract." In a hurry to "fall in love," "be married" or "get out of a bad situation," we again and again fall prey to our worst nightmare by connecting with someone without processing their baggage and our baggage, thus ending up in a relationship that continues to poison and hurt us forever. Thus, in the very fabric of such a relationship is the reality of divorce.

The principles of marriage and family must rest upon commonality of a basic kind that seeks to covenant with an individual in marriage who is like ourselves. That is, their temperament and nature must be understood and compatible, sharing the basic matters of sexuality and spirituality in common. To do otherwise is to end up in a futile cycle of fix and fake, ever trying to bring the other person into commonality and a common emotional expression so that our lives can celebrate together what we know and feel. God took the rib from Adam and called it Eve and gave it back again. He received from the Lord that which God had taken from him and gave it back again. Eve was bone of his bone and flesh of his flesh, if only each of us could share in our mating such commonality. This is the ideal and the thing that we should seek from the Father. When the joy of commonality can be celebrated in our lives, we can truly say, "what God has joined" and when it isn't we must never speak of that which is not as if it were.

One plus one equals one.
In our confusion we chose an opposite.
Ever since, we, him or her have tried to fix, faking
the difference measured by endurance.
No commonality equals no common-union.
No communion equals confusion and
restlessness.
Covenant marriage is in the heart –
Custom fit from the start.
Minds that click, joy unspeakable,
Soul-mates a natural flow,
Chemistry that dances with every move –
commonality can't be faked!

I am you and you are me.
The Father alone makes it three.
Words forever flow as minds run free,
What grace and rest anoints our way as we
surrender our posturing and dance with truth!

No more pretending but confrontation –
No more hiding – declaring the truth.
No more being controlled but free, commonality is
a gift from God.
We rest our minds and hearts overflow with love,
our bodies and spirits celebrate, we are one!

Those who do not build marriage on commonality, end up in their latter years cynical, angry, bitter, very unhappy and unfulfilled. Look around you and observe. To hang on to a shadow marriage for money, reputation, the law, for the children, or to satisfy others, is to commit emotional suicide and spiritual frustration. Grace sets us free from ourselves to declare that Christ is the provider of a second chance.

CHAPTER FIFTEEN

TILL DEATH DO US PART

"Wives, submit yourselves unto your own husbands, as unto the Lord. For the husband is the head of the wife, even as Christ is the head of the church: and he is the savior of the body. Therefore as the church is subject unto Christ, so let the wives be to their own husbands in everything. Husbands, love your wives, even as Christ also loved the church and gave himself for it. ... So ought men to love their wives as their own bodies. He that loveth his wife loveth himself. For no man ever yet hateth his own flesh; but nourisheth and cherisheth it, even as the Lord the church. ... For this cause shall a man leave his father and mother, and shall be joined unto his wife, and they two shall be one flesh" (Ephesians 5:22-31).

One of the primary reasons Dancing With Broken Feet was written was to encourage all who have built shadow marriages on agendas of their own making which could not nurture or grow because they were of their own making, have no commonality or depth. Divorce was written into the very fabric of such relationships, leaving them stranded. Usually one is in denial and the other is in emotional chaos. After living through the routine of fake or fix, they settle into the emptiness of their daily routines because of the fear of change. This more often than not leads one party to an affair mentally, while the other locks into the emptiness of "That's just the way it is" mind-set. This is especially true if there is a sexual connection from time to time, and food on the table. The male often is easily deluded by this unreality. In such dead-end street, shallow marriages are typical in this highly sex oriented culture. The light of reality and a desire to be free usually happens when one or the other comes to terms with his or her lostness or discovers God's grace and purpose. Dancing With Broken Feet seeks to strengthen individuals in transition, those who have come to terms with the inability of the bondage created by their wrong choices. The pain of failure and the inability to fix, brings a second chance, an opportunity to build a covenant marriage and a GRACE family upon commonality and God's grace.

With God's help and right thinking, coupled with detailing and processing, a man or woman, though broken and dysfunctional, can come to know the joys of a relationship where the man loves the wife as Christ loved the church and the wife holds her husband in respect with love. Though this reality is rare in our world, it is still God's order. The church spoken of here is not a place but a people for whom Christ died. We, who have trusted God's grace in Jesus Christ, are the church. The reality of loving someone as Christ loved the church declares that Christ, who knows all our sins and failures, loves us as a cherished bride. Thus the man should love his wife with full knowledge of her and the details of her life.

Therefore it is most important that two people come to know each other inside and out through processing and detailing their lives and discovering their commonality. Having missed out on this the first time, they must determine to live, learn and walk with the Lord. Thus, discovering wonderful possibilities that can be lived out, if they are willing to change and learn from past failures. Couples who determine to walk in a covenant marriage have a great opportunity to help others, as they demonstrate the reality of a GRACE family.

This book has little to say to those not willing to change, as difficult as change may be. My prayer is that for each woman who reads this book, that she with her second chance in life and love may walk with a man in commonality, and truly be loved as Christ loved the church while bringing her sexuality, blessed by grace to a loving, caring, processed relationship. My prayer for all the men who read this book is that as God gives them a second chance, they will bring to the relationship their spirituality on fire with grace.

Growing inside a processed relationship, loved and respected by a woman who will walk with the heart, as he becomes her covering. Together, both men and women must learn to confront one another with love and honesty while allowing their hearts to be blended by the detailing of their lives, without posturing or game playing of any kind.

Life is too short and change is absolutely essential as the Father teaches us, who are broken and to keep growing and living in the joy and fulfillment of His grace. What God joins and is allowed to maintain, no man can put asunder. When the heart dances with grace and truth, men and women alike are set free. Marriage is not a piece of paper but a reality of the heart. Find that reality, dancing not with perfection and expectation but with love and forgiveness afire in the human heart. If you always do what you have always done, you will always get what you always got. Pray that the Father will grant you the willingness and the power to change and to walk free to your good and His glory by His grace!

A PRAYER OF ONE WITH BROKEN FEET

Dear Father,
You have loved us while we were yet sinners. You found us broken and have given us hope. We pray that You will teach us to love. Failure was written into our former relationship. Help us write victory into or second chance as we learn to give and receive love.

Father, help us to change without fear of failure. Teach us to process every detail of our lives, trusting Your ability and power within us. May we learn to walk in covenant with one another. As men, may we love as Christ loved the church and as women may we learn to receive and respect.

Anoint our days with grace and truth. In covenant, help us to forget the past and be free. Learning from our failures, never to repeat them, keeping our eyes on Jesus, His death, burial and resurrection with our feet on the ground. May the GRACE family be the home of our new beginnings. May we walk together in His love till death do us part!

In Jesus' name So-Be-It

BONUS MATERIAL

Download your free bonus marriage worksheet/chart here:

https://goo.gl/qHTR8D

Study it carefully. Understand it and use it daily. Your marriage will be greatly blessed!

OTHER WORKS BY DANNY GRIFFIN

- **<u>Living Waters, Empty Wells and Holy Dippers</u>**
  Danny's work in India

- **<u>Born To War</u>**
  From birth to maturity of the believer

- **<u>For Those Who Ask</u>**
  Ambassadorial evangelism

- **<u>I Must Say</u>**
  A poetic parody by Ismael Footfahrt

- **<u>Freedom Drive</u>**
  The story of Carolina Christian Ministries, day school, fellowship and how it came to be

- **<u>Her!</u>**
  Thoughts on love, romance and intimacy in poetic form

For information on how to obtain any of the above visit:
http://www.SpiritualMaintenance.org/Books.html

BOOKS BY RON MCRAY

- The Last Days
- Through The Water, Through The Fire
- Behold, I Am Making All Things New
- Behold, I Am Coming Quickly
- Pearls Of Great Price
- What In The "World" Happened Between 30 A.D. And 70 A.D?
- The Lazarus Affair: A novel
- Did Jesus Have Long Hair?: The Biblical Verdict
- The Heavens Declare The Glory Of God: A Lost Understanding Of The Ancient Zodiac
- Was Jesus 3 Days And 3 Nights In The Heart Of The Earth?
- Satan, The Devil And The Adversary
- 666 And The Anti-Christ Of Revelation
- God Came Riding On A Cloud
- The Good Life: A Biblical Understanding Of Being Spirit Filled
- Is It Wine Or Is It Grape Juice?
- The LORD Is Not Slack: Did God Keep His Promises... On Time?
- And We Think GOD Doesn't Talk To Us?
- The Judean Social Life
- Israel In Perspective
- Seeking Truth: The Scope And Sequence Of The Bible
- Are You In The Eternal Kingdom Of YAHWEH?
- Don't Worry About It Right Now
- Prophecy In 2017

15 Book Series:

<u>Things That Your Preacher Forgot To Tell You!</u>

1. Righteousness Apart From Salvation: In The 1st Century
2. Is The Church The "ekklesia" Of The Bible?

3. Who Saw Jesus And When Did They See Him From His Cruci-fixion To His Ascension – And Why Is This So Important?
4. Are There Three Heavens – Or More?
5. Is It Appointed Unto Man Once To Die?
6. The Relationship Of The Church, The Kingdom And House To Eschatology
7. A Study Of Old Testament Prophets And Their Fulfillment
8. How To Interpret The Book Of Revelation Consistently
9. The Sign Of The End Revealed (Matthew 23,24,25)
10. Things That Were "About To Happen" In   The Days Of Jesus And His Disciples
11. Someone Changed My Bible!
12. Ephesians: Not The Book That You Thought That It Was
13. The Lord's Supper
14. First-Born And Second-Born: A Study Of Types and Anti-types
15. The Writings Of Jesus Revealed!

DVD'S BY DR. RON MCRAY

- Introduction To Eschatology
- Why Am I Here – What Is My Purpose?

Use this link to access the website for all information concerning books

www.EschatologyReview.com

Toll-free ordering 1-888-393-5933

Made in the USA
Columbia, SC
02 May 2018